FASCSM

SETH H. PULDITOR

MASON CREST
PHILADELPHIA

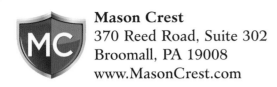

Mason Crest
370 Reed Road, Suite 302
Broomall, PA 19008
www.MasonCrest.com

Printed and bound in the United States of America

CPSIA Compliance Information: Batch #MEG2012-4. For further information, contact Mason Crest at 1-866-MCP-Book.

First printing
1 3 5 7 9 8 6 4 2

Library of Congress Cataloging-in-Publication Data

Pulditor, Seth H.
  Fascism / Seth H. Pulditor.
     p. cm. — (Major forms of world government)
  Includes bibliographical references and index.
  ISBN 978-1-4222-2139-6 (hc)
  ISBN 978-1-4222-9456-7 (ebook)
  1. Fascism—Juvenile literature. I. Title.
  JC481.P84 2013
  321.9'4—dc23
                                    2012027898

TITLES IN THIS SERIES

COMMUNISM   MILESTONES   MONARCHY
DEMOCRACY   IN THE EVOLUTION   OLIGARCHY
DICTATORSHIP   OF GOVERNMENT   THEOCRACY
FASCISM

TABLE OF CONTENTS

Introduction   4

    by Dr. Timothy Colton, Chairman
    Department of Government, Harvard University

1 Destroying Democracy 7

2 What Is Fascism? 20

3 The Nazis' Rise to Power... 30

4 The Approaching Storm 39

5 Nightmares Made Real 48

Chapter Notes   58

Chronology   60

Glossary   61

Further Reading   62

Internet Resources   62

Index   63

Contributors   64

INTRODUCTION by Dr. Timothy Colton, Harvard University

When human beings try to understand complex sets of things, they usually begin by sorting them into categories. They classify or group the phenomena that interest them into boxes that are basically very much alike. These boxes can then be compared and analyzed. The logic of classification applies to the study of inanimate objects (such as, for example, bodies of water or minerals), to living organisms (such as species of birds or bacteria), and also to man-made systems (such as religions or communications media).

This series of short books is about systems of government, which are specific and very important kinds of man-made systems. Systems of government are arrangements for human control and cooperation on particular territories. Governments dispense justice, make laws, raise taxes, fight wars, run school and health systems, and perform many other services that we often take for granted. Like, say, minerals, bacteria, and religions, systems of government come in a wide variety of forms or categories.

Just what are those categories? One of the earliest attempts to answer this question rigorously was made in the fourth century BCE by the brilliant Greek philosopher Aristotle. His study *Politics* has come down to us in incomplete form, as many of his writings were lost after he died. Nonetheless, it contains a simple and powerful scheme for classifying systems of government. Aristotle researched and illustrated his treatise by looking at the constitutions of 158 small city-states near the eastern shores of the Mediterranean Sea of his day, most of them inhabited by Greeks.

According to Aristotle's *Politics*, any system of government could be accurately classified and thus understood once two things were known. The first was, how many people were involved in making political decisions: one person, a small number, or a large number. The second issue was whether the system was designed to serve the common good of the citizens of the city-state. Taken together, these distinctions produced six categories of governmental system in all: monarchy (rule by one civic-minded person); tyranny (rule by one selfish person); aristocracy (rule by the few in the interests of all); oligarchy (rule by the few to suit themselves); constitutional government or "polity" (rule by the many in the common interest); and finally a form of mob rule (rule by the many with no concern for the greater good).

The fifth of these classic categories comes closest to modern representative democracy, as it is experienced in the United States, Western Europe, India, and many other places. One of the things Aristotle teaches us, however, is that there are many alternatives to this setup. In addition to the volume on democracy, this Mason Crest series will acquaint students with systems of government that correspond in rough terms to other categories invented by Aristotle more than two thousand years ago. These include monarchy; dictatorship (in Aristotle's terms, tyranny); oligarchy; communism (which we might think of as a particular kind of modern-day oligarchy); fascism (which combines some of the characteristics of tyranny and mob rule); and theocracy (which does not fit easily into Aristotle's scheme, although we might think of it as tyranny or oligarchy, but in the name of some divine being or creed).

Aristotle focused his research on the written constitutions of city-states. Today, political scientists, with better tools at their disposal, delve more into the actual practice of government in different countries. That practice frequently differs from the theory written into the constitution. Scholars study why it is that countries differ so much in terms of how and in whose interests governmental decisions are taken, across broad categories and within these categories, as well as in mixed systems that cross the boundaries between categories. It turns out that there are not one but many reasons for these differences, and there are significant disagreements about which reasons are most important. Some of the reasons are examined in this book series.

Experts on government also wonder a lot about trends over time. Why is it that some version of democracy has come to be the most common form of government in the contemporary world? Why has democratization come in distinct waves, with long periods of stagnation or even of reverse de-democratization separating them? The so-called third wave of democratization began in the 1970s and extended into the 1990s, and featured, among other changes, the collapse of communist systems in the Soviet Union and Eastern Europe and the disintegration of differently constituted nondemocratic systems in Southern Europe and Latin America. At the present time, the outlook for democracy is uncertain. In a number of Arab countries, authoritarian systems of government have recently been overthrown or challenged by revolts. And yet, it is far from clear that the result will be functioning democracies. Moreover, it is far from clear that the world will not encounter another wave of de-democratization. Nor can we rule out the rise of fundamentally new forms of government not foreseen by Aristotle; these might be encouraged by contemporary forms of technology and communication, such as the Internet, behavioral tracking devices, and social media.

For young readers to be equipped to consider complex questions like these, they need to begin with the basics about existing and historical systems of government. It is to meet their educational needs that this book series is aimed.

Benito Mussolini addresses a crowd in Rome, 1930s. The sign behind him includes the Latin inscription *arx omnium nationum* ("the center of all nations"), a phrase used by the ancient statesman Cicero to describe the seat of the Roman Empire. Mussolini dreamed that his Fascist government would restore Italy to the glory once known by ancient Rome.

DESTROYING DEMOCRACY

Benito Mussolini would always portray the 1922 March on Rome as an epic event. Answering his call, legions of armed men—300,000 strong—had assembled at four points across Italy. With Mussolini out in front, four massive columns of disciplined fighters had trekked through the countryside and converged on the capital city. Confronted with this irresistible force, Italy's weak and inept government had buckled. Mussolini took the reins of power. His bold act saved the country from chaos. His heroic leadership put Italy on the path to glory.

It was a compelling story, and one that Italians heard often as Mussolini tightened his grip on power during the 1920s and 1930s. But it was a story that had almost no basis in reality. The March on Rome wasn't anything like the high drama depicted in official propaganda. It had played out as farce.

LEGACY OF THE FIRST WORLD WAR

By the early 1920s, Italian society simmered with discontent. The country's economy was in shambles. High unemployment and rising prices made life difficult for millions of people. Class divisions bred antagonism and anxiety. Wealthy landowners were at odds with peasants who wanted to form agricultural unions. In some areas, poor peasants seized farms. In the industrial sector, factory owners tried to keep wages low. But workers responded with strikes. They also took over plants, mines, and warehouses. This stirred up fears of communism, an economic and political system that promised the elimination of private property. A revolution had recently brought Communists to power in Russia. Many Italians worried that a similar revolution might take place in their own country.

Adding to Italy's troubles was the legacy of World War I, which erupted in August 1914 and finally ground to a halt in November 1918. Most of the fighting took place in Europe, along front lines that in many cases didn't move more than a few hundred yards for months on end, despite appalling casualties. Trench warfare and the use of weapons such as poison gas and the machine gun led to slaughter on a scale never before witnessed. The total number of dead will never be known with certainty. Most historians accept a figure of around 10 million. An additional 20 million or more were wounded in the conflict.

World War I would have far-reaching consequences beyond the shocking toll in killed and maimed. In addition to Russia's tsar, the war swept away the monarchies and dissolved the empires of three defeated states. Even in countries that had fought on the winning side, public revulsion at the brutality and apparent senselessness of the conflict was widespread. Many people lost faith in existing social and political institutions.

In Italy, considerable resentment of the government grew out of the war. Italian forces had suffered a string of defeats. About 1.5 million

Italian soldiers had been killed or wounded. Yet it was hard to see what their sacrifice had achieved. In the peace negotiations that followed the fighting, the so-called Big Three victorious nations—the United Kingdom, France, and the United States—largely ignored Italy's interests, even though Italy had fought on their side. Italy received little in the way of new territory. Many Italians saw this as a national humiliation.

As a group, Italy's war veterans were especially frustrated and angry. On returning to civilian life, many found themselves unable to get a job.

FOUNDING OF THE FASCIST MOVEMENT

Benito Mussolini found a way to channel the anger of veterans for his own political gain. A journalist, he had served in the Italian army during the war. In March 1919, in the city of Milan, he cofounded the Fasci Italiani di Combattimento (Italian Combat Leagues). This political movement was made up of people from different walks of life but included many veterans. Mussolini formed his followers into paramilitary units called *squadristi*. They

Historians credit an Italian poet, nationalist, and war hero named Gabriele D'Annunzio (1863–1938) with establishing the roots of fascism in Italy. In 1919 D'Annunzio led a small army to capture the city of Fiume (present-day Rijeka, Croatia). D'Annunzio believed that this port on the Adriatic Sea, which had a large population of ethnic Italians, should be part of Italy. The short-lived independent government he established in Fiume would inspire Italy's later Fascist government under Mussolini.

Mussolini adopted the fasces, a bundle of rods with an ax head sticking out, as the symbol for his Fascist movement. He was deliberately trying to invoke the glory of the Roman Empire. In ancient Rome, the fasces was a symbol of authority.

would become known as Blackshirts, from the color of their uniform tops.

The political agenda put forth by the Fasci Italiani di Combattimento included a strong dose of nationalism. It called for Italy's territorial expansion. The western coast of the Balkan Peninsula was the area of greatest interest. Many ethnic Italians lived there. Those people had to be brought within the borders of Italy, Mussolini said.

If this sort of nationalism hinted at the aggressive foreign policy Mussolini would pursue once in power, early on there was little to suggest that his movement threatened democracy.

Italy's experience with democratic governance was fairly new. A constitutional monarchy with an elected parliament had been established only in 1870. That was the year Italy's unification from various smaller states was completed. Italy's budding democracy had never functioned especially well. Too often the country's various political parties were unable to find common ground and compromise. The political divisions became more pronounced after World War I.

Nevertheless, the Fascist Manifesto of 1919 proposed to deepen Italian democracy. It called for lowering the voting age from 21 to 18. It also called for women to be given the right to vote—a very liberal idea for the time. The manifesto also backed worker rights, such as a minimum wage and an eight-hour workday. Provisions such as these, in addition to a call for a high tax on wealth, didn't endear Mussolini to Italy's political conservatives, its business elite, or its rich landowners.

Mussolini ran for Italy's parliament in late 1919, but he lost. After that, the Fascist movement became much more clearly identified with conservative elements of Italian society. Alliances were formed with the business community and with landowners. And Blackshirts undertook a fearsome campaign of violence and intimidation. They attacked socialists. They terrorized leaders of trade unions. They battled the paramilitary fighters of Italy's Communist Party. The threat of communism would be one of Mussolini's constant themes.

INEFFECTUAL GOVERNMENTS

In parliamentary elections in 1921, Mussolini and some of his followers won seats. Mussolini officially created the Partito Nazionale Fascista (National Fascist Party). The Fascists were invited to participate in a governing coalition headed by Prime Minister Giovanni Giolitti of the Liberal Party. Mussolini accepted. The Fascists were still a minor party, however. They held just 35 of the 535 seats in Italy's parliament.

Mussolini soon helped bring Giolitti's government down by pulling out of the governing coalition. Another government was formed—this time without the participation of the Fascists—but it quickly fell. In February 1922, the Liberal Party's Luigi Facta set up another coalition government.

In July, a national strike was called by the Socialist Party and a union representing railway workers. Mussolini declared that if Facta's government didn't break up the strike, his Fascist Party would. And that's what happened. With the regular workers off the job, Blackshirts took over. They kept rail transportation and other essential services operating. Within a week, the strike was over. This won the Fascists much support among middle-class Italians.

Italy's troubles, however, only got worse. Worker unrest continued. There were riots in the cities. In the countryside, poor peasants battled wealthy landowners. Italy appeared to be sliding closer and closer toward chaos.

PHANTOM MARCH

On October 24, 1922, the Fascist Party held a national meeting in Naples. At that meeting, Mussolini stoked fears of a coup. "Either the government will be given to us," he declared, "or we shall seize it by marching on Rome."

Blackshirts were soon moving toward the capital—by train. But Mussolini's threat to seize the government was a bluff. The Blackshirts were a ragtag bunch. Some were armed only with farm implements. And they numbered perhaps 20,000—one-fifteenth the total that Mussolini would later claim had participated in the March on Rome. The Blackshirts remained well outside the capital. They didn't dare risk a direct confrontation with Italy's army, against which they would have been badly overmatched.

Mussolini himself stayed in Milan, more than 350 miles north of Rome. If the government called his bluff, he could escape to safety across the border with Switzerland.

Prime Minister Luigi Facta was prepared to call Mussolini's bluff. But Italy's king, Victor Emmanuel III, was not. The king feared a civil war. He also worried about a Communist revolution. Victor Emmanuel decided that his country needed a strong government that would restore order.

Mussolini leads the March on Rome, 1922.

That was exactly what Mussolini promised. So on October 29, the king telegraphed Mussolini in Milan. He offered the Fascist leader the position of prime minister.

Mussolini had gotten what he wanted. But he insisted on going through with the "March on Rome" anyway. He took the overnight train from Milan, arriving just outside the capital on the morning of October 30. There he joined his Blackshirt followers, who had also covered the final miles to Rome by train. With Mussolini and several of his top aides taking the lead, the Fascists paraded into the city as photographers snapped away. Many of the photos conveyed a sort of heroic grandeur. Viewing them, one would hardly suspect that the March on Rome had actually been a short stroll.

IL DUCE

Two liberal parties, the Socialist Party and the Italian People's Party, held the most seats in Italy's parliament. Victor Emmanuel's intention was to lock these left-wing parties out of government. He wanted Mussolini's Fascists to lead a coalition of right-wing parties. The idea was popular with many ordinary Italians as well.

Mussolini did, in fact, form a right-wing coalition government. But he viewed power sharing as a temporary measure only. He planned to concentrate all authority in his own hands.

A first step involved changing Italy's election law. Seats in parliament had always been awarded according to the proportion of the vote each party received. If a party got 5 percent of the vote, for example, it was awarded 5 percent of the seats. If it received 10 percent of the vote, it got 10 percent of the seats. But in 1923, Italy did away with proportional representation. According to a new law Mussolini succeeded in getting passed, any party that received 25 percent of the vote was awarded two-thirds of the seats in the parliament.

In advance of elections held in April 1924, Mussolini's Blackshirts unleashed a vicious campaign of violence and voter intimidation. They claimed a landslide at the polls, gaining a two-thirds majority in the

> Mussolini's Blackshirts served as the inspiration for the Sturmabteilung Brownshirts of the German Nazi Party.

parliament. Immediately afterward, Mussolini moved to eliminate all opposition. He took the title *Il Duce*, meaning "the Leader."

Two years later, in 1926, all political parties except for the Fascist Party were outlawed. Opposition newspapers were banned. Mussolini had established the world's first fascist government.

DESPERATE TIMES IN GERMANY

Benito Mussolini's rise to power inspired another would-be leader who dreamed of restoring his nation to greatness: Adolf Hitler. Born in Austria in 1889, Hitler had enthusiastically enlisted in the German army at the outbreak of World War I. The end the war left him bitter and disillusioned. He refused to believe Germany had been defeated on the battlefield. Instead, he insisted, the country had been "stabbed in the back" by disloyal elements on the home front—especially liberal politicians, Jews, and Communists.

None of this was true. By late 1918, Germany's military situation had indeed been hopeless. But the victorious Allies never forced the German army to officially surrender. So Hitler could believe the myth that Germany might have won the war if not for the treachery of unpatriotic members of society. It was a myth he would later spread—and one that many Germans would come to accept.

Germans already had plenty of reasons to be bitter about World War I. The war had claimed the lives of at least 1.7 million German soldiers. In the Treaty of Versailles—the 1919 peace agreement formally ending the conflict—the Allies imposed harsh and humiliating conditions on defeated Germany. Significant pieces of German territory were given to other countries. Germany also lost all of its overseas colonies. Germany was forced to accept sole responsibility for starting the war, and the size of its armed forces was strictly limited. An especially burdensome section of the treaty required Germany to compensate other countries for the costs of the war. These reparations were enormous. The payments contributed to the ruination of Germany's economy. In the early 1920s, unemployment spiked to nearly 25 percent. Inflation became so severe that Germany's currency, the Mark, lost value by the hour, and a wheelbarrow filled with Marks wasn't even enough to buy a newspaper. Germans' life savings simply evaporated.

POLITICAL TURMOIL

World War I had swept away the government of Wilhelm II, the German Kaiser, or emperor. In place of the old German monarchy, a democratic

This group of German soldiers in World War I includes one who would become fascism's most infamous leader: Adolf Hitler (front row, far left). Hitler served on the western front and was twice decorated for bravery in battle. Like many Germans, he was bitter that German leaders had signed an armistice in November 1918 while the German army still held territory in France and Belgium. However, Hitler's belief that German soldiers had been "stabbed in the back" ignored the truth of Germany's strategic situation in the fall of 1918.

government had been set up. It was known as the Weimar Republic, from the city where Germany's new constitution was drafted, in 1919.

From the outset, however, the Weimar Republic faced huge difficulties. Many Germans refused to support the new government. Some opposed the very idea of representative democracy, a form of government that was virtually unknown in the German political tradition. Many conservative Germans wanted to see a member of the royal family restored to power. At the other end of the political spectrum were radicals who favored a Communist system. In between these two extremes were a host of factions with varying political beliefs and goals. Many had little interest in sharing power, which is critical to the success of any democracy.

Germany in the years after the war saw multiple assassinations and attempted revolutions. In cities such as Berlin and Munich, bloody street battles between rival factions raged regularly.

One group that often took part in these violent clashes was the Sturmabteilung (German for "Storm Division"). Sturmabteilung (SA) members were called Brownshirts. They made up the paramilitary force of the National Socialist German Workers Party. History, however, remembers the party better by a shortened name: the Nazis.

Adolf Hitler had joined the forerunner of the Nazi Party, which was a small and marginal group, in late 1919. His mesmerizing skills as a speaker helped boost party membership. Hitler called for Germany to reject the Treaty of Versailles. He said all Germans should be united under a strong government. But, ominously, he said that no one who was Jewish could be a German.

BEER HALL PUTSCH

In July 1921, Hitler became head of the Nazi Party. His title was *Führer*. In German that means "leader."

By late 1923, Nazi Party membership had swelled to perhaps 30,000. Hitler decided it was a good time to make a power grab similar to Mussolini's March on Rome. His scheme, though, was rather harebrained. Backed by several hundred of his Brownshirts, Hitler would burst in on a

Some of the Nazi Brownshirts who tried to seize power in Munich during the failed 1923 putsch.

political rally inside a Munich beer hall. There he would proclaim a revolution. Three top leaders in the government of the German state of Bavaria were going to be at the rally, and Hitler would get their approval for his uprising. While all this was going on inside the beer hall, a larger force of Brownshirts would surround the Munich army barracks. The Brownshirts would convince the soldiers to join the revolution. Then they would all march to Berlin and topple the Weimar government.

The so-called Beer Hall Putsch began on the evening of November 8, 1923. (A putsch is a sudden attempt to overthrow a government.) Unfortunately for Hitler and the Nazis, the soldiers refused to go along with the revolution. And while Hitler was distracted, the Bavarian government officials escaped from the beer hall. They ordered army reinforcements to Munich.

Still, on November 9, Hitler and 3,000 Nazis decided to march on the army headquarters in Munich. Police blocked their way in a narrow street. A brief gunfight erupted. When it was over, 16 Nazis and three policemen lay dead. Hitler fled but was arrested a couple days later.

Hitler and other Nazi Party members involved in the putsch were charged with treason. They were found guilty. Hitler could have been sentenced to life in prison. Instead, he received a sentence of just five years.

RACE AND HATE

Hitler served his time at a Bavarian prison called Landsberg. It wasn't exactly hard time. He had a large, comfortable cell. He also enjoyed special privileges. He could entertain visitors whenever he wanted. Hitler passed his days in the company of other Nazi Party members who were serving time at Landsberg.

Hitler also began writing a book while in prison. He dictated the text to his private secretary, Rudolf Hess. The book was called *Mein Kampf* ("My Struggle"). The first volume would be published in 1925. The second volume would come out the following year.

In *Mein Kampf*, Hitler told his life story. Or, more exactly, he told an idealized version of his life story. He also gave his views about Germany's problems. He singled out Communists and Jews for much of the blame. Hitler's anti-Semitism, or hostility toward Jewish people, was apparent throughout his book. He spoke of Jews in the most hateful terms. He said they were the enemies of civilization. He accused them of trying to control the world. And he said they were inferior.

Hitler's anti-Semitism was part of a much-broader racism. He divided all people into racial groups, which he ranked according to their "higher or lesser value." The lowest races, Hitler said, were "chaff." (*Chaff* means something that is worthless.) In addition to Jews, Hitler put Slavs—including Poles, Russians, Ukrainians, and Czechs—in that category. Later the Nazis would add the Roma (Gypsies), "Asiatics," and Africans to their list of the racially inferior. And they would refer to these people as "subhuman."

According to Hitler, nearly all of humanity's achievements could be credited to a "master race." He called this race the Aryans. In the distant past, the Aryans had conquered and enslaved "lower human types." And this was the way it should be, Hitler believed. It was through the enslavement of lesser peoples that the master race advanced culture.

Eventually, however, the Aryan masters and the conquered peoples began to intermarry. This, Hitler said, had brought disaster. It had lowered the "racial level" of the Aryans. "The Aryan," Hitler wrote, "gave up the purity of his blood. . . . He became submerged in a racial mixture and gradually lost his cultural creativeness."

Hitler was vague about the exact origins of the Aryans. But he did say that modern Germans were their descendants. Hitler called Germans the "highest species of humanity on this earth." As the "master race," they had the right—even the duty—to take whatever they needed from supposedly inferior peoples. Physically, Hitler said, true Aryans could be distinguished by their fair skin, blond hair, and blue eyes.

Hitler's racial ideas weren't supported by science. They were, in fact, complete nonsense. But those who waded through *Mein Kampf* should have had great reason for concern. Hitler was more than a ranting bigot. He offered a chilling plan for remaking Germany. The plan involved destroying the Weimar Republic. The Nazis hated democracy because it promoted equality for all citizens, including so-called inferior peoples. Hitler's plan called for forcibly maintaining Aryan racial purity within Germany. There would also be wars with France and the Soviet Union. And there would be *Lebensraum*, or living space, for an expanding German population. This would come at the expense of the Slavic peoples to the east.

Mein Kampf sold poorly when it was first released. Thus, very few people in Germany or the rest of the world understood the true scope of the threat presented by the Nazis.

Hitler ended up serving only nine months of his sentence for treason. He was released from Landsberg Prison in December 1924. He was more determined now to destroy the Weimar Republic and bring his version of fascism to Germany.

2

WHAT IS FASCISM?

Fascism never gained the reach of other types of government. As of January 2011, not a single one of the world's 194 countries could accurately be called a fascist state. By contrast, 115 countries qualified as democracies, according to Freedom House. (Freedom House is an organization that promotes political freedom and human rights. It is based in Washington, D.C., and funded by the U.S. government.)

At the peak of its influence, in the 1930s and early 1940s, fascism was the governing philosophy in only a handful of countries. So why study it? For one thing, fascism helped bring about the most destructive war in history. Unspeakable atrocities were committed under the influence of its ideas. And small pockets of supporters continue to champion some of those ideas.

AN ELUSIVE DEFINITION

What exactly is fascism? It might seem surprising, but scholars cannot agree on a precise definition.

Several factors help account for this. Unlike other political philosophies, fascism was never systematically described by its advocates. Fascists stressed action over analysis. In fact, according to many scholars, contempt for intellectual pursuits is itself a characteristic of fascism. Fascist leaders almost always sought to motivate their followers with emotional rather than rational appeals. "Feelings," Nazi propaganda minister Joseph Goebbels famously declared, "have to take the place of thinking." As a result, even basic questions such as what were fascism's core goals can be open to interpretation.

Furthermore, circumstances varied in the countries generally regarded as fascist. The policies of their leaders differed, sometimes in important ways. What, then, should be considered the essential elements of fascism, and what should be considered incidental differences among fascist regimes? Creating a definition of fascism that is

Mussolini addresses an enormous crowd at a rally, 1930s. Fascist leaders like Mussolini and Hitler used their public appearances to establish a "cult of personality." In fascist states, the leader is presented as the one individual who can save the nation from its problems. Through propaganda, the leader is portrayed as a person who cannot make mistakes and who always acts in the best interests of the entire nation.

broad enough while still meaningful can be maddeningly difficult. For example, aggression toward other nations is widely thought to be a major characteristic of fascist states. Certainly, Germany under Hitler and Italy under Mussolini displayed such aggression. But Spain under Francisco Franco did not. Still, Franco's regime—which Italy and Germany helped bring to power—is often thought of as fascist. Many scholars resolve this difficulty by saying that fascism reached its *full* development only in Germany and Italy. Other scholars insist that, while deeply influenced by fascism, Spain under Franco wasn't in fact fascist.

There is yet another hurdle standing in the way of a precise definition of fascism. Important characteristics of fascism are by no means unique to fascism. Take, for example, the cult of leadership. In fascist states, the leader (always a dictator) was built up as a near-mythic figure. His greatness, according to the official propaganda, knew virtually no bounds. He held the solution to all the nation's problems. The people had only to follow him. Of course, dictators of all stripes have sought to portray themselves in similar terms.

Or take the use of secret police. All fascist regimes spied on their own people and stamped out dissent through networks of secret police. Nazi Germany had the Gestapo, Fascist Italy the OVRA (Organization for Vigilance and Repression of Anti-Fascism). In Portugal, the fascist-leaning dictator António de Oliveira Salazar used the Gestapo as a model in creating his State Defense and Surveillance Police. Again, however, fascists weren't alone in terrorizing their populations with secret police. Secret police are a common feature in many authoritarian forms of government, including communism.

To gain and hold on to power, fascists sought to organize large numbers of people into a mass movement. Fascism is based on single-party rule. But these characteristics, too, also apply to communism.

CHARACTERISTICS OF FASCISM

Despite the difficulty of defining fascism with precision, most (but not all) scholars agree on the broad outlines. They point to a cluster of features that, taken together, set fascism apart from other forms of government and other political philosophies. The following are some of the most significant of those features.

Supremacy of the state. Under fascism, the needs of the state (as determined by the leader) take priority over all else. Fascism denies that individuals have any rights that the state is obligated to respect. Rather, individuals exist to serve the state. And the state demands their obedience. Dissent isn't tolerated. It is regarded as treason.

Under fascism, there are no clear lines between public and private behavior. The state seeks as much control as possible over all aspects of people's lives. "The only person who is still a private individual in Germany," noted Nazi labor official Robert Ley, "is somebody who is asleep."

Mussolini offered a slogan to express the all-embracing nature of the state under fascism: "Everything in the State, nothing outside the State, nothing against the State." This is a pretty good description of totalitarianism. That term—first popularized by Mussolini and his education minister, the philosopher Giovanni Gentile—describes a political system in which the state exercises nearly unlimited authority. Most scholars agree that totalitarianism is a goal of fascism. In practice, Mussolini's Italy never came close to becoming a totalitarian regime. Nazi Germany, on the other hand, did.

Extreme nationalism. Fascism assumes that one's own nation is superior to others. At the very least, this belief produces racist attitudes. At worst, it can be used to justify repression of, or aggression against, supposedly inferior peoples.

> "THE FASCIST CONCEPTION OF LIFE STRESSES THE IMPORTANCE OF THE STATE AND ACCEPTS THE INDIVIDUAL ONLY IN SO FAR AS HIS INTERESTS COINCIDE WITH THOSE OF THE STATE."
>
> —BENITO MUSSOLINI AND GIOVANNI GENTILE, "THE DOCTRINE OF FASCISM" (1932)

For fascism, the attainment of national glory is of primary importance. One requirement for this is ensuring the "purity" of the nation. And to fascists, "nation" doesn't mean the same thing as "country." According to the Nazis, "Aryans" made up the authentic German nation. Jews were among the people who couldn't be true Germans, even if they happened to be citizens of Germany. Fascists in Italy took a somewhat broader, less racially based view of national purity—at least at first. Mussolini was willing to accept all citizens of Italy as authentic Italians, provided they gave their allegiance to the Fascist Party. Fascism, in his view, would mold the distinct ethnic groups into a unified Italian nation. Eventually, however, Mussolini introduced measures that stripped Italy's Jews of their citizenship. But he did so merely as a means of promoting an alliance with Nazi Germany.

Fascism attaches an almost mystical importance to the unity of the nation. It assumes that the nation has a collective spirit or will. This isn't an idea that stands up to rational scrutiny. A nation is composed of a great many people. They have different hopes, different beliefs, and different goals. Obviously, there can never be full agreement among all the members of a

As the Nazi Party gained power, it launched a national boycott of Jewish-owned businesses. The sign in this 1933 photo reads, "Germans, defend yourselves, do not buy from Jews." The soldier pictured is a member of the Sturmabteilung (SA), or "Brownshirts"—the paramilitary wing of the Nazi Party.

nation. But under fascism, the leader is said to embody the national spirit. The leader is said to express the authentic will of the people. And what he decrees is not to be questioned.

Culture of violence. Violence was a key factor in the rise of fascism. Attacks by fascist paramilitary groups—like the SA in Germany and the Blackshirts in Italy—silenced critics and intimidated political rivals. But violence also played a more indirect role in bringing fascists to power. Continual fighting in the streets (which fascists were largely responsible for) gave citizens the impression that their societies were descending into chaos. Fascists offered a solution. They promised to restore law and order. People who might not otherwise have supported the fascists did so in the hopes they would make good on this promise.

But fascists didn't give up paramilitary violence once they had taken over governing. Potential opponents still had to be intimidated into silence. Others needed to be gotten rid of entirely.

Authoritarian governments often require violence (or at least the threat of violence) to sustain them. And, in many cases, even democratic governments have been established only after violent struggles. The American Revolution is but one example. So the fact that fascists used violence to gain and hold on to power doesn't set fascism apart from other forms of government.

In one respect, however, the place of violence within fascism is quite unusual. For fascists, violence isn't just a means to get or keep power. Rather, it's an end in itself. Fascism regards violence as a way to cleanse and renew the nation. It doesn't matter whether the target is a foreign country or a supposedly disloyal group at home. Fascism glorifies struggle. It sees conflict as both inevitable and desirable. "War is to men," Mussolini declared, "as maternity [motherhood] is to women." José Antonio Primo de Rivera, the founder of Spain's fascist Falange Party and an admirer of Mussolini, echoed that view. "War," he said, "is inalienable from man. . . . It is an element of progress. It is absolutely necessary!" Hitler, too, saw the world in similar terms. "Those who want to live," he

LOOKING TO THE PAST

The fascist regimes that came to power did so in societies that were in the midst of social, economic, or political turmoil. In short, these societies weren't functioning smoothly. Under the circumstances, it might seem odd that fascists would proclaim the superiority of their own nation. But they did. And they often looked to the past to support their claims. Mussolini conjured up the grandeur of the Roman Empire. Hitler and the Nazis invoked not one but two *Reichs*, or empires: the medieval empire established by Charlemagne and the empire established by Chancellor Otto von Bismarck following the unification of Germany in the early 1870s. These periods, in the view of the Italian and German fascists, were golden ages for their respective peoples. The Roman Empire and the two German Reichs boasted great cultural, economic, and military achievements. They were the most powerful European states of their time. This, the fascists said, was proof of an inherent national greatness.

So what had happened? Where, during the 1920s, was the national greatness of the German and Italian people? Hitler and Mussolini both pointed a finger at liberal democracy. They believed that individual rights and majority rule undermined a heroic national spirit. Hitler also singled out Jews. He said they "contaminated" the blood of the Aryan race. He blamed Jews, along with liberals, for selling out Germany at the end of World War I. Germany's defeat in that conflict had brought an end to the Second Reich.

Fascism promised a national rebirth. It would renew the greatness of the culture. It would recapture the glories of the past. And fascist leaders left little doubt that this would be achieved through military conquest.

Mussolini offered promises of a new Italian empire that would assume the mantle of ancient Rome. Hitler and the Nazis established the Third Reich. They claimed that the new German empire would last for a thousand years.

wrote, "let them fight, and those who do not want to fight in this world of eternal struggle do not deserve to live."

An economic "third way." Fascists—whether in Italy, Spain, Germany, or elsewhere—won support by promising to stamp out the threat of communism. Fascism has always been fiercely anti-communist. But that doesn't mean fascists championed free-market capitalism, communism's economic opposite. On the contrary, they often identified capitalism as an ill of modern society. Capitalism, they said, fostered greed and materialism. It exploited the working class. It interfered with the natural unity of the nation.

Fascists endorsed a "third way" in economic policy. It was supposed to be a middle course that included aspects of capitalism and aspects of socialism. Fascists upheld the idea of private property, a foundation of capitalism. But, to a significant degree, they also championed government direction of the national economy and—in theory—the rights of workers. These are hallmarks of socialism.

The specifics of fascist economic policy varied considerably

Fascists in Italy and Germany often used the specter of outside threats, such as a takeover by Communists or Jews, to encourage voters to elect their candidates. This poster from 1932 features two Nazi Brownshirts. The text says that the Nazis are making sacrifices to create a new Germany, and it asks people to vote for the party in an upcoming election.

by country. In Italy, Mussolini tried an approach known as corporatism. Under this system, labor unions were done away with. In their place, state-organized industry and trade "corporations" were set up. These were basically associations of workers and employers involved in the same economic activity. Each corporation also included Fascist Party officials in key roles. Representatives of all the corporations met in the national Council of Corporations. Eventually, it replaced the Italian parliament as the country's main legislative body. Corporatism allowed the state to exercise control over the economy while ownership of business and industry was kept in private hands. It was supposed to eliminate conflict between workers and employers. Labor issues would be resolved through cooperation. Workers would be assured of fair treatment.

Germans participate in a Hitler Youth rally, 1930s. The Hitler Youth was an organization created by the Nazi Party as a way to instill in young people Nazi beliefs and ideals.

In Germany, the Nazi regime attempted to exert tighter control of the economy. It largely decided which goods were to be produced, set wages and prices, and dictated working conditions. Labor unions were banned. Business owners were expected to serve the "national interest," as defined by the leader. "The state," Hitler said, "should retain supervision and each property owner should consider himself appointed by the state. It is his duty not to use his property against the interests of others among his own people. . . . The Third Reich will always retain its right to control the owners of property."

Scholars have noted the wide gap between what fascists said about economic policy and what they actually did. In both Italy and Germany, workers' interests

The Nazi Party held annual rallies at Nuremberg, Germany, in which hundreds of thousands of people participated.

were ignored. A cozy relationship evolved between the state and business. Large firms—especially in Germany—reaped huge profits making weapons under government contract. Economic policy under fascism, notes the historian Robert O. Paxton, "tended to be driven by the need to prepare [for] and wage war. Politics trumped economics."

3

THE NAZIS' RISE TO POWER

By the time of his release from prison in December 1924, Adolf Hitler recognized that the Nazi Party wasn't nearly strong enough to take power by force. So he settled on a different strategy. The party would temporarily work within Germany's democratic system. It would act like a legitimate political party. Nazis would campaign for seats in Germany's parliament, the Reichstag. The party would slowly build its base of support with the German people.

To gain loyal followers for the future, Hitler focused on winning the hearts and minds of young Germans. To this end, the Nazis established youth organizations. Boys were allowed to join the Hitler Youth. For their female counterparts, there was the League of German Girls. Both organizations included activities such as hiking, camping, and sports. But they were nothing like German versions of the Boy Scouts or Girl Scouts. Members of the Hitler Youth and the League of German Girls received constant instruction in the Nazis' poisonous racial ideas. They were taught about Aryan superiority and the wickedness of Jews. They were told it was their duty to maintain the racial purity of the German nation. They were also drilled in the importance of complete obedience to the Nazi Party and its Führer, Adolf Hitler.

In addition to establishing the youth organizations, Hitler set up a new security force in 1925. It was called the Schutzstaffel, or SS. At first, the SS was a small unit whose purpose was to protect the Führer. It was part of the much-larger SA, the Nazis' storm trooper force. But the SS would eventually become independent of, and more important than, the SA. Its members were among Hitler's most fanatical and brutal followers. SS units would carry out some of the worst atrocities committed by the Nazis.

MORE ECONOMIC SETBACKS

During the years 1925–1928, Germany enjoyed relative calm. The economic situation had improved. Unemployment was way down. With loans from the United States, Germany's war debts had been restructured. In this environment, the Nazis' extreme message failed to attract many people. In national elections for the Reichstag held in May 1928, the Nazi Party got only about 2.5 percent of the vote.

But in late October 1929, the U.S. stock market crashed. This set off a disastrous chain of events. The world was plunged into a decade-long economic crisis called the Great Depression.

In Germany, unemployment rose steadily. With the country no

> Originally, membership in the Hitler Youth and the League of German Girls was voluntary. But after coming to power in the 1930s, the Nazis made membership a requirement. All youngsters who were ethnically German and between the ages of 10 and 18 had to be enrolled in one of the youth organizations.

longer able to pay its debts, the Weimar government raised taxes. This made the situation even worse. Growing numbers of Germans sank into desperate poverty. Crime spiked. German society appeared to be coming apart at the seams.

Paul von Hindenburg decided to take action. Hindenburg was Germany's president. Under the Weimar constitution, the president had several ways to influence the Reichstag. But he couldn't control the legislative process.

The Nazi Party attracted followers by promising to build a glorious new Germany. This propaganda poster from the early 1930s includes the slogan "Hitler builds, we help."

As head of state, the president was responsible for appointing Germany's chancellor. The chancellor served as head of government, much like the prime minister in a British-style parliamentary system. Once appointed by the president, the chancellor formed a government by choosing the cabinet—the officials in charge of the major government ministries. The constitution required that all cabinet ministers be deputies in the Reichstag. Other than that, the chancellor could choose whomever he wished for his cabinet—at least in theory.

In reality, there were two major limitations on the chancellor's ability to pick the cabinet he wanted. First, because the Reichstag could bring down the chancellor's government through a no-confidence vote, the chancellor had to choose a cabinet that would win the support of a majority of deputies in the Reichstag. So unless the chancellor's party held a majority of seats in the Reichstag (which never happened), the chancellor had to form a coalition with other parties. In exchange for their support in the Reichstag, these parties received cabinet posts for their members.

The second major check on the chancellor's freedom to pick a cabinet came from the president. Under the Weimar constitution, the president had the authority to dismiss the chancellor or members of the cabinet. In practice, this meant that the chancellor needed to get the president's approval for his cabinet.

The president also had the power to dissolve the Reichstag. That is what Hindenburg decided to do in 1930, amid Germany's mounting economic and social problems. He called new elections for September of that year.

QUEST FOR THE CHANCELLORSHIP

The Nazis ran an effective campaign. Hitler's skill as a public speaker was a huge asset. And now, many distressed Germans were receptive to the Nazi message. That message was vague about policy details. It was designed to play on emotions rather than appeal to reason. Thus, Hitler stoked German pride and nationalism by promising to build up the armed forces and restore Germany's glory. He channeled Germans' anger by offering scapegoats, or people to blame, for the country's problems. Those scapegoats were the supposedly corrupt Weimar Republic leaders and the Jews. Hitler raised fears that Communists would take over the government. He suggested that strong leadership under the Nazi

> ### KEY IDEA
>
> Nationalism is loyalty to one's own cultural, ethnic, or national group—particularly when the interests of one's group come into conflict with the interests of other groups.

Party would bring order, unify the German people, and provide jobs for the unemployed.

The Nazis began receiving financial support from many of Germany's wealthiest industrial leaders. These industrialists included the owners of steel and armaments companies. They stood to reap profits if the Nazi Party came to power and began a military buildup.

The Nazis received more than 18 percent of the vote in the 1930 elections. This gave them more seats in the Reichstag than all but one of the other 13 parties that had won seats. Through cooperation and compromise with other parties, the Nazis could have tried to become part of a governing coalition. But Hitler had no interest in sharing power. He held democracy in contempt. Nazi Party deputies did their best to disrupt the Reichstag's work. That wasn't difficult. The other parties were prone to constant bickering.

With its gridlocked legislature providing no solutions, Germany's problems got worse. And again, the Nazis were doing their part to make sure the trend continued. SA storm troopers brought violence and lawlessness to many German cities, especially Berlin. They harassed and beat up opponents of the Nazi Party. They vandalized newspaper offices and assaulted editors. They fought pitched street battles with Communists on a regular basis. And the police were unable or unwilling to stop the SA.

All the while, the Nazi Party kept up a steady stream of propaganda. The propaganda campaign—which was directed by Joseph Goebbels—included the party's usual themes. But now Goebbels emphasized two messages in particular. The first message was that the Communists were growing ever

KEY IDEA

Communism is an economic and political system whose stated purpose is to do away with private property, social classes, and inequality. Under communism, the resources needed to produce goods are supposed to be owned by all members of society.

more dangerous. They were, according to the Nazis, on the brink of seizing power. The second message concerned the greatness of Adolf Hitler. He was depicted as the one person who could save Germany.

Growing numbers of Germans believed that message. Paul von Hindenburg wasn't one of them. The president had met the Nazi Führer in early 1931. He'd quickly concluded that Hitler was unfit for high office.

But Hindenburg's seven-year term as president was set to expire in April 1932. With his 85th birthday approaching, Hindenburg planned to retire. But he eventually decided to seek reelection. Hindenburg

Paul von Hindenburg (1847–1934), a German hero of World War I, was elected president of the Weimar Republic in 1925. Though he disliked Hitler, Hindenburg was unable to prevent the Nazi Party from gaining seats in the Reichstag.

was worried that Hitler might run for, and win, the presidency. Hitler did decide to run for president. While Hindenburg ended up winning by a comfortable margin, Hitler succeeded in further raising his profile among the German people.

Right after the election, Chancellor Heinrich Brüning banned the SA and the SS. But this didn't stop the Nazis' march toward power, as Brüning hoped.

Disorder continued to reign in the Reichstag. Brüning was forced to resign in late May 1932. On the advice of Kurt von Schleicher, a former general and close adviser, Hindenburg appointed a little-known politician named Franz von Papen as the new chancellor. Schleicher thought Papen was weak. But that's exactly what he wanted. As defense

The German nobleman Franz von Papen (1879–1969) helped Hitler become chancellor in 1933, believing that the Nazi leader could be easily controlled. However, the Nazis made sure that Papen had no influence in government. After his arrest by Nazi SS troops in a 1934 purge, Papen resigned as vice chancellor.

minister, Schleicher intended to be the real power behind the Papen government.

Like so many others at the time, Schleicher was worried about the growing turmoil in Germany. He wanted the government to be strict, strong, and stable. He wanted the chancellor to have more power and the Reichstag to have less. And for that to happen, he believed he needed the cooperation of Adolf Hitler. So Schleicher had made a secret deal with the Nazi leader. Hitler agreed not to oppose the Papen government. Schleicher promised to have the ban on the SA and SS lifted.

Schleicher didn't like the Nazis. He had no desire to see them gain power. But he believed he would be able to outmaneuver and even control Hitler. He was wrong.

After Papen's government failed to get any support in the Reichstag, Hindenburg dissolved the legislature. Elections were called for July 1932. In the run-up to the voting, the SA and SS—legal once again—unleashed more street violence than ever. And the Nazi Party received more support from the German people than ever. Over 37 percent of German voters cast their ballots for the Nazis. This gave Hitler's party 230 of the Reichstag's 608 seats. That was more than the next two parties combined. The Social Democratic Party of Germany got 133 seats. The Communist Party of Germany got 89.

Hitler declared that the Nazi Party wouldn't participate in any coalition unless he was made chancellor. Hindenburg refused to agree to this, however. Almost as soon as the new Reichstag convened, it was dissolved. Yet another round of elections was scheduled for November.

This time, the Nazis didn't fare quite as well. They received 33 percent of the vote. While that was still more than any other party, the Nazis lost 34 seats in the Reichstag. The Social Democratic Party also lost seats. The Communist Party, on the other hand, gained. It now had 100 seats.

Again, Hitler demanded the chancellorship. Again, Hindenburg refused. But Papen couldn't find enough support in the Reichstag to form a governing coalition. This opened the way for Schleicher. On December 2, 1932, he became chancellor.

Papen felt betrayed by Schleicher. He decided to team up with Hitler to take down the new chancellor. Papen and Hitler began secretly bargaining over how they would share power in a coalition government.

Behind the scenes, Hitler's cause was also being championed by Germany's wealthy elite. German business leaders, bankers, and industrialists sent a petition to Hindenburg. It urged the president to appoint Hitler chancellor.

"WITH PRIDE WE SEE THAT ONE MAN REMAINS BEYOND ALL CRITICISM, THAT IS THE FÜHRER. THIS IS BECAUSE EVERYONE FEELS AND KNOWS: HE IS ALWAYS RIGHT, AND HE WILL ALWAYS BE RIGHT. THE NATIONAL SOCIALISM OF ALL OF US IS ANCHORED IN UNCRITICAL LOYALTY, IN THE SURRENDER TO THE FÜHRER THAT DOES NOT ASK FOR THE WHY IN INDIVIDUAL CASES, IN THE SILENT EXECUTION OF HIS ORDERS. WE BELIEVE THAT THE FÜHRER IS OBEYING A HIGHER CALL TO FASHION GERMAN HISTORY. THERE CAN BE NO CRITICISM OF THIS BELIEF."

—RUDOLF HESS

KEY IDEA

In democratic societies, the "will of the people" is expressed through periodic elections. Fascists sneer at the democratic process, however. They deny that governance should reflect the preferences of a majority of citizens. In the fascist state, the leader determines the will of the people.

Hindenburg finally gave in after Schleicher was unable to win support in the Reichstag. He asked for Schleicher's resignation. Then, on January 30, 1933, Hindenburg named Hitler to the chancellorship. The aging president believed the Nazi Führer would be kept in check by his cabinet. Papen was to serve as vice chancellor. In addition, only two of the remaining nine cabinet posts would go to Nazis.

Adolf Hitler had risen to power through the democratic process. Now he and the Nazis quickly set to work destroying German democracy.

THE END OF THE WEIMAR REPUBLIC

On the night of February 27, 1933, flames engulfed the Reichstag building. The fire had been deliberately set by SA storm troopers, but the Nazis said the blaze was the work of a Communist conspiracy. On February 28, Hitler convinced Hindenburg to sign an emergency decree to deal with the supposed threat. The decree suspended all civil rights that Germans were guaranteed by the Weimar constitution.

The Nazis used the decree to suppress all opposition, Communist or otherwise. Germany's transformation into a fascist state was nearly complete.

4

THE APPROACHING STORM

By late March 1933, only a month after the Reichstag fire, Adolf Hitler wielded absolute power in Germany. He convinced President Hindenburg to sign a decree that permitted the arrest of anyone who criticized the Nazi Party or the German government. Hitler also bullied members of the Reichstag into passing the Enabling Act. It gave him, as chancellor, the authority to issue laws. He didn't need the approval of the Reichstag or the president. The Enabling Act even gave Hitler the authority to ignore the constitution. He pledged to use these new powers sparingly. That proved to be an empty promise.

The Nazis immediately set up Germany's first concentration camp, at Dachau. The first inmates were political opponents of the Nazis, such as Communists, members of the Social Democratic

Smoke billows from the Reichstag, February 27, 1933. Though it had been set by Brownshirts, Hitler and the Nazis claimed that the Reichstag fire was the work of a Communist conspiracy. Hitler used the fire as a pretext to seize power under an emergency decree.

Party, and liberal Catholics. Concentration camp prisoners toiled long hours at forced labor. They were subjected to brutal punishments. And they were never told when, if ever, they would be released.

OFFICIAL ANTI-SEMITISM

The Nazis soon turned their attention to Germany's Jews. On April 1, 1933, Joseph Goebbels organized a nationwide boycott of Jewish-owned businesses.

Less than a week afterward, Hitler issued the first in a series of laws marginalizing Jews. "The Law of the Restoration of the Civil Service" made "Aryanism" a requirement for public-sector positions. Jewish professionals ranging from doctors and lawyers to university professors lost their jobs. Another law placed restrictions on Jewish children in the public schools.

Before the end of 1933, the Nazis had taken control of all the country's newspapers. All Jewish journalists were fired.

Jews were also forbidden to work in theater productions or movies. Jewish artists were banned from showing their works. Jewish writers couldn't be published.

Throughout 1934 and early 1935, anti-Semitism in Germany simmered. Jewish businesses and synagogues were vandalized. SA and Nazi Party members randomly harassed and beat up Jews on the streets.

In September 1935, the Nazi leadership further isolated the Jewish community with two measures known as the Nuremberg Laws. The Reich Citizenship Law stripped Jews of German citizenship. The Law for the Protection of German Blood and German Honor sought to ensure Aryan "racial purity." Among other restrictions, it prohibited Jews from marrying persons "of German or kindred blood."

The Nuremberg Laws introduced a problem of classification. Who, exactly, should be considered Jewish? For the Nazis, the question had little to do with religious practice. Rather, it was a matter of race—or, at least, what the Nazis mistook to be race? But at what point did "Jewish blood" make someone racially Jewish. Was a person with three "Aryan" grandparents and one Jewish grandparent German or Jewish? Eventually, the Nazis set guidelines. A person with three or four Jewish grandparents was considered a full Jew. So was a person with two Jewish grandparents, if certain other conditions were met (for example, if the person was married to a Jew). Otherwise, persons with two Jewish grandparents were classified as *Mischlinge* (mixed-blood Jews) of the first degree. Persons with one Jewish grandparent were classified as Mischlinge of the second degree. They were relatively fortunate. While they suffered discrimination, they would not later be systematically murdered—unlike full Jews and Mischlinge of the first degree.

The Nuremberg Laws weren't the only fateful development that occurred in Germany in 1935. That year, Hitler decided to launch a massive effort to rearm Germany. German factories began churning out ships, planes, tanks, and artillery pieces. Hitler also announced plans to increase the size of the German army to more than half a million men. All of this violated the terms of the Treaty of Versailles. But the international community failed to take action to curb the German military buildup.

OTHER FASCIST MOVEMENTS

By the mid-1930s, fascist movements or fascist-influenced governments had arisen in a number of countries besides Italy and Germany. For example, Portugal had the Estado Novo (New State) government of dictator

BURNING BOOKS

On May 10, 1933, the German Student Association and the Nazi Party's propaganda ministry staged a nationwide spectacle. In some three-dozen German cities, university students lit huge bonfires. Into those fires they threw thousands of copies of what they called "nation-corrupting books and journals."

The book burning was the climax of a six-week campaign billed as an "Action Against the Un-German Spirit." The organizers claimed that German culture—especially the country's language and literature—had been debased. The culprits included modernist and avant-garde (experimental) writers, socialists, foreigners, and especially Jews. The German Student Association demanded that these influences be eliminated from the school curriculum. The students wanted every German university to be "a stronghold of the German *Volk* [Folk] tradition and a battleground reflecting the power of the German mind."

Apparently, the students didn't think the German mind could handle certain ideas. On May 10, the works of Communist thinkers such as Karl Marx, Friedrich Engels, and Leon Trotsky were burned. Also targeted were books by authors considered sympathetic to socialism. They included the British writer H. G. Wells and Americans John Dos Passos, Theodore Dreiser, Helen Keller, Jack London, John Reed, and Upton Sinclair. All the works of Sigmund Freud, the Austrian-born father of psychoanalysis, were relegated to the fires. The reason? The Nazis said Freud's emphasis on humans' unconscious desires was "soul-shredding." Thomas Mann was a German writer who had won the Nobel Prize in Literature. But his books were burned because he'd criticized the idea of dictatorship. The works of Erich Maria Remarque, another well-regarded German writer, were also burned. Remarque had vividly described the human toll of World War I in his novel *All Quiet on the Western Front*. The classic novel *A Farewell to Arms*, by American Ernest Hemingway, was burned for the same reason.

Thousands of books smolder in a huge bonfire as Germans give the Nazi salute, 1933.

The book burnings of May 10 signaled the coming of harsh censorship measures in Germany. Under the Nazis, even discussing certain ideas wouldn't be tolerated. Joseph Goebbels, the Nazi minister of propaganda, hailed this elevation of ignorance. "The age of arrogant . . . intellectualism," Goebbels proclaimed at the Berlin book burning, "is now at an end! . . . [The German people] are doing the right thing at this midnight hour—to consign to the flames the unclean spirit of the past. . . . Out of these ashes the phoenix of a new age will arise."

THE GESTAPO

A totalitarian regime such as Nazi Germany seeks to control all aspects of citizens' lives. This includes not simply what people do, but what they say and even what they think. To root out any possible opposition, totalitarian regimes often rely on secret police organizations. In Nazi Germany, this meant the Gestapo.

The Gestapo was officially formed in April 1933. Its agents were chosen for their zeal and loyalty to the Nazi Party.

At its peak, the Gestapo had about 40,000 agents. That's a relatively small number, given that Germany's population topped 60 million by the mid-1930s. But Gestapo agents wore plain clothes. And each agent recruited ordinary citizens to act as informers. As a result, Germans could never be sure when someone might be spying on them. And even the mildest of complaints about conditions in the country or about Nazi policies or leaders could land a person in great trouble.

The Gestapo had unlimited authority to deal with Germans suspected of disloyalty. The legal system offered citizens no protections, such as access to a lawyer or the right to a trial. Many people were arrested, brutally tortured, and executed by the Gestapo.

António de Oliveira Salazar. He drew inspiration from Mussolini. Chile had the Movimiento Nacional Socialista (National Socialist Movement), which closely followed ideas espoused by Nazi Germany. Even Great Britain had a sizeable fascist movement. Led by Sir Oswald Mosley, the British Union of Fascists claimed a peak membership of 50,000. It would finally be outlawed after the outbreak of World War II.

Neither these nor any of the various other fascist movements and quasi-fascist governments that took shape during the 1930s and early 1940s ever developed into the kind of full-fledged fascism seen in Nazi Germany or Fascist Italy. Why that would be the case is a question political scientists and historians of fascism have often struggled to answer. There is broad consensus that fascism—because it strongly rejects individual rights and limited government—has little chance of succeeding in any country with a long tradition of liberal democracy. Some scholars point to other cultural factors that might have predisposed Italy and Germany to a full embrace of fascism. Germany, to take but one example, exalted militarism (especially among the Junker aristocracy of Prussia) long before the Nazis came to power. Even the personal qualities of Mussolini and Hitler may explain, at least in part, why fascism reached its full development in Italy and Germany but not elsewhere. Both men were much more charismatic than, say, Portugal's Salazar or Spain's Franco.

EARLY BATTLEGROUNDS OF FASCISM

In October 1935, Italian forces invaded Ethiopia. Soldiers from that East African country fought bravely. But they were poorly equipped. Their old rifles proved no match for Italy's airplanes, tanks, artillery, and machine guns. By May 1936, the fighting was over. The Ethiopians had been crushed.

In Italy, Mussolini was hailed as a hero. And he basked in the glory. "Italy at last has her empire," he told an ecstatic crowd in Rome. "It is a Fascist empire because it bears the indestructible sign of the will and power of the . . . Fasces of Rome."

Fascists were soon at the center of another conflict. It broke out in Spain in July 1936.

Both Mussolini and Hitler had great personal charisma and were talented public speakers. These characteristics enabled them to fully establish fascist states in Italy and Germany.

For several years, Spain had witnessed considerable unrest. There were labor strikes, riots, and even a pair of armed uprisings inspired by socialists.

In early 1939, parliamentary elections brought to power a left-wing coalition called the Popular Front. It included members of the Communist Party of Spain, the Spanish Socialist Workers Party, the Republican Left, and other liberal parties.

In response to the victory of the Popular Front, a right-wing political coalition was formed. It was called the National Front. Among its smallest members was the Spanish Falange, which had received less than 1 percent of the vote. The Falange was an explicitly fascist party. It sought to create a Spanish state modeled after Mussolini's Italy.

Suspicion of the Popular Front helped draw growing numbers of Spanish people to the Falange's message. By early summer 1936, the party had perhaps 40,000 members.

Meanwhile, a group of army generals was planning to overthrow Spain's government. Among the plotters was General Francisco Franco.

On July 12, Falange gunmen murdered an anti-fascist army officer. The next day, a leading conservative politician was assassinated in retaliation. The conservative generals decided that the time had come to act. They launched their coup attempt on July 17.

The generals expected to seize power quickly. But they were thwarted. What followed was a bloody and brutal civil war. It pitted the forces of the elected left-wing government, the Republicans, against pro-fascist and conservative Nationalist rebels.

Both sides received aid from beyond Spain's borders. The Communist Soviet Union sent weapons and military advisers to the Republicans. Otherwise, no foreign government directly supported the Republicans. But citizens from several dozen countries—including the Soviet Union, England, France, the United States, and Mexico—volunteered to fight on the Republican side. Many of these volunteers wanted to take a stand against fascism. Many were Communists. In all, about 60,000 foreign volunteers fought with the Republicans.

Franco's Nationalists, however, received much more foreign support. Most of it came from fascist and pro-fascist countries. Pro-fascist Portugal sent 12,000 regular army troops. Fascist Italy contributed tanks, aircraft, and about 75,000 soldiers. Nazi Germany sent more than 15,000 men, along with hundreds of tanks and planes. The Nazi leadership saw the Spanish civil war as an opportunity to test new equipment and tactics. German air operations proved especially effective in the conflict.

In April 1939, after nearly three years of bitter fighting, the Spanish civil war finally ended. Franco's Nationalists, and fascism, had won. Perhaps half a million people were dead as a result of the war.

But a much deadlier and more horrific conflict was fast approaching. That conflict would be ignited by the terrible ambitions of Adolf Hitler.

Ruins of the village of Belchite, which was destroyed in a 1937 battle during the Spanish civil war. After the war the fascist-leaning dictator of Spain, Generalissimo Francisco Franco (1892–1975), decided that the village would not be rebuilt. He wanted the ruins to stand as a monument to the dangers of communism.

5

NIGHTMARES MADE REAL

Between 1936 and 1939, as the Spanish civil war raged, more ominous developments were occurring in Germany and Italy. For the most part, the rest of the world failed to appreciate the significance of these developments. Time after time, the threat posed by fascism was underestimated.

BLOODLESS EXPANSION

On October 25, 1936, Italy and Germany signed a treaty of friendship. The alliance between the two fascist states was known as the Rome-Berlin Axis.

Hitler had long dreamed of uniting all German-speaking peoples under the Third Reich. More than 6.5 million German-speakers lived in Austria. Since 1934, the fascist Fatherland Front had ruled that country, which borders both Germany and Italy. But the Fatherland Front had taken its cues from Mussolini rather than Hitler. And it sought to maintain Austrian independence.

Austria had a Nazi Party. It favored union with Germany.

Throughout 1937, Germany applied pressure on the Austrian government to agree to union. By early 1938, Hitler was issuing thinly veiled threats to bring Austria into the Third Reich by force if necessary. Kurt Schuschnigg, Austria's chancellor, decided to put the issue before his country's citizens. A vote to determine Austria's political future was scheduled for March 13. On March 11, Hitler informed Schuschnigg that Germany would invade unless Schuschnigg turned power over to the Austrian Nazi Party. Schuschnigg refused to do so. But he did resign. The Austrian Nazis quickly seized control of important government ministries. They cancelled the scheduled vote.

On March 12, German troops rolled across the border into Austria. They met no resistance. Instead, they were greeted by cheering crowds. The *Anschluss*, or union of Austria with Germany, had been achieved.

Hitler soon turned his attention to another area with a large German-speaking population: the Sudetenland region of Czechoslovakia. He claimed that the Czech government mistreated the more than 3 million ethnic Germans who lived there. By the summer of 1938, Hitler was threatening a German invasion of Czechoslovakia.

Neville Chamberlain, the British prime minister, wanted to find a peaceful solution. On September 15, Chamberlain met with Hitler at the Führer's mountaintop villa in Bavaria. Hitler said he wanted the Sudetenland turned over to Germany. Chamberlain made no promises. But after returning to Britain, he convinced his cabinet to accept Hitler's proposal. He also obtained the approval of France. With few options, the government of Czechoslovakia agreed as well.

On September 22, Chamberlain met with Hitler again. He told

> Germany and Italy dubbed their alliance the Axis because they said the whole world would rotate on the decisions they made.

Hitler that the Sudetenland would, in fact, be turned over to Germany. To Chamberlain's astonishment, Hitler said that wasn't good enough anymore. He now insisted on a German military occupation of the Sudetenland, to begin by October 1. Further, he demanded that everyone who wasn't ethnically German be expelled from the region. There was no way the government of Czechoslovakia could agree to those conditions. Allowing large numbers of German troops to enter the Sudetenland was practically an invitation for Hitler to invade the entire country. A dejected Chamberlain returned to London.

France, Great Britain, and Czechoslovakia began preparing for war. But Chamberlain still hoped for a peaceful resolution. A conference was arranged. It took place in Munich on September 29. In attendance were Chamberlain, Hitler, Mussolini, and Édouard Daladier, the prime minister of France. Representatives of the Czechoslovakian government had also traveled to Munich. But Hitler refused to let them participate in the talks.

After several hours of discussions, the leaders signed the Munich Agreement. It gave Hitler everything he'd demanded regarding the Sudetenland. In return, Hitler promised to make no further demands for territory.

Chamberlain was confident that Hitler would be true to his word. "I believe it is peace for our time," the British prime minister said upon returning home.

In reality, the appeasement at Munich hadn't ensured peace. It

The Nazis believed that certain people were "unfit" to live. Such people included anyone with a physical disability, mental illness, or Down syndrome. For the purpose of maintaining racial "hygiene" (health), the Nazis killed Germans with these conditions.

The program began in October 1939, with physically disabled infants and children up to three years old. It was soon expanded to include older children and adults. An estimated 200,000 people were eventually killed under the program.

had simply postponed war. Hitler hadn't given up his plans for Lebensraum, the additional "living space" he believed Germans needed and deserved. Now, though, he was convinced that Great Britain and France were weak-willed and would do almost anything to avoid a war. "Our enemies are little worms," Hitler told a group of German generals about a week after the Munich conference.

CONTINUING MISTREATMENT OF JEWS

For Jews living under fascist rule, conditions were going from bad to worse. In July 1938, under the influence of his Nazi allies, Mussolini issued the Manifesto of Race. This was a series of laws targeting Italy's Jewish community. Up to this point, Jews in Italy hadn't been discriminated against officially. The new laws stripped Jews of Italian citizenship.

Participants at the 1938 peace conference in Munich included (from left) Prime Minister Neville Chamberlain of Britain, Prime Minister Edouard Daladier of France, Hitler, and Mussolini. Although Daladier was concerned about the territorial ambitions of the fascist leaders, he agreed to Chamberlain's "appeasement" policy.

They prohibited Jews from marrying non-Jewish Italians. They removed Jews from all government positions. Jews were no longer allowed to be teachers. Jewish students were expelled from schools.

In Germany, about 17,000 Jews of Polish ancestry were suddenly rounded up in late October 1938. They were expelled from the country. They took with them only what they could carry.

In Paris, France, a 17-year-old Jewish youth whose family had been expelled from Germany lashed out. On November 7, he shot an official at the German embassy. The official died two days later.

The Nazis used the incident as an excuse to unleash a nationwide attack on Jews in Germany. On the evening of November 9, members of the SS, the Hitler Youth, and other Nazi Party thugs went on a rampage.

After 1933, the Nazi Party gradually took rights away from German Jews. By late 1938 the government was beginning to implement a program intended to remove Jews from German territory. This would eventually become the so-called Final Solution—an attempt to exterminate all of Europe's Jews. These German Jews are prisoners in a concentration camp at Sachsenhausen, December 1938.

As police stood by and watched, the Nazi mobs assaulted and, in some cases, murdered Jews. They burned down synagogues. They ransacked Jewish-owned stores. They smashed so many windows that the incident would become known as *Kristallnacht*, or the Night of Broken Glass.

> ## KEY IDEA
>
> Genocide is the deliberate and systematic destruction of a racial or cultural group.

As if the Jewish community hadn't suffered enough, the Nazi government forced Jews to pay for all the damage. The Nazis also arrested and sent as many as 25,000 Jewish men to concentration camps. Within a month, a decree made it illegal for Jews in Germany to own businesses.

COUNTDOWN TO WORLD WAR II

By early 1939, Hitler had set his sights on taking the remainder of Czechoslovakia. It was just six months since he'd promised Neville Chamberlain that Germany had no interest in acquiring more territory.

Under the threat of a massive German invasion, the president of Czechoslovakia reluctantly surrendered his country. German army units streamed into Czechoslovakia unopposed on March 15, 1939.

The British and French governments protested. They declared Germany's seizure of Czechoslovakia a clear violation of the Munich Agreement. They refused to recognize the legality of the German occupation of Czechoslovakia. Yet neither country took action to reverse that occupation.

However, Britain and France did draw a line in the sand. To the east of Germany and north of Czechoslovakia lay Poland. The British and French governments declared that any German aggression against Poland would be a cause for war with Germany.

Shortly after the German invasion of Czechoslovakia, Mussolini decided to expand his Italian empire. On April 7, 1939, Italian forces invaded Albania. In less than a week, they had overrun the small country.

German troops invade Poland, September 1939. Aggression by the fascist leaders during the 1930s led to the Second World War.

The following month, Mussolini and Hitler signed the "Pact of Steel." This agreement set up a formal political and military alliance between Germany and Italy. The two fascist countries would fight together in the war both of their leaders knew was coming soon. A third powerful state, Japan, would join the Axis Powers in 1940.

Hitler hated communism. He hated the Soviet Union. But he didn't want to risk a war with that huge Communist country—at least not yet. Germany was planning an invasion of Poland. This could well plunge the Third Reich into a war with Britain and France. Hitler didn't want to fight a third powerful enemy at the same time. On August 23, 1939, Germany and the Soviet Union signed a nonaggression pact. Under the treaty, the two countries pledged not to fight each other for a period of 10 years. The Germans and Soviets also reached a secret agreement. Germany would allow the Soviet Union to take eastern Poland, as well as three small states on the Baltic Sea: Estonia, Latvia, and Lithuania.

For the Nazis, everything was now in place. On September 1, without warning, German forces launched a massive invasion of Poland. Two days later, Britain and France declared war on Germany. World War II was under way.

FASCISM ON THE MARCH

In the first year of the war, the Nazis appeared unstoppable. They over-ran Denmark, Norway, the Netherlands, Belgium, and Luxembourg. With the surrender of France in June 1940, Germany was in firm control of Western Europe. Only the British held out. In July, the German air force began a months-long campaign to bomb Britain into submission.

Turning to the east, Hitler's troops swept into Romania. Italy, mean-while, invaded Greece. Hungary voluntarily joined the Axis Powers.

During the first months of 1941, Germany occupied Bulgaria. Nazi forces also invaded Yugoslavia. In the western part of that country, the Independent State in Croatia was set up. It was ruled by the Ustasha. The members of this fascist group had much in common with the Nazis. Their beliefs were shaped by racism. They hated the multicultur-alism of Yugoslavia and sought an ethnically pure Croatia. The Ustasha

JAPANESE FASCISM?

Among Japanese scholars, the question of whether Imperial Japan during the late 1930s and early 1940s should be considered a fascist state generates heated controversy. At the very least, however, Japan displayed many characteristics associated with fascism.

For example, it had a highly aggressive foreign policy, complete with wars of conquest. Japan's leaders encouraged the notion of Japanese national superiority. Individuals were expected unquestion-ingly to serve the needs of the state. While the emperor, Hirohito, wasn't a hands-on dictator in the mold of Hitler or Mussolini, he was said to embody the Japanese national spirit. He was also said to be infallible.

established concentration camps to imprison and kill Serbs, Gypsies, and Jews.

Fascist movements would crop up in nearly all of the other countries of Eastern Europe during the war. Few, however, were as vicious as the Ustasha.

As the summer of 1941 began, Hitler double-crossed the Soviet Union. Breaking the 1939 nonaggression pact, Germany launched a massive invasion on June 22. The shocked Soviet forces retreated in chaos. Over the next two months, the Germans advanced eastward along a broad front extending from the Baltic Sea in the north to the Black Sea in the south.

Special SS units followed the German army's advance. They were called the *Einsatzgruppen* ("Special Task Forces"). Their task was to murder Jews in the conquered territory. This was part of what the Nazis termed the "Final Solution"—a plan to kill all of Europe's Jews.

The Einsatzgruppen shot most of their victims. But for the Nazis, this wasn't efficient enough. They set up a network of concentration camps and death camps. Jews from all the countries the Nazis occupied were rounded up and sent to these camps. Those who were young and strong enough performed slave labor until they died of illness or exhaustion. The others were immediately murdered with poison gas. All told, the Nazis' systematic killing of Jews, called the Holocaust, would claim about 6 million lives. About 3 million non-Jews would also be killed in

Millions of people were killed in concentration camps during the era of Nazi rule in Germany.

the concentration and death camps. They included Poles, Gypsies, Soviet prisoners of war, and others.

LOOKING BACK

By December 1941, the German campaign against the Soviet Union had bogged down. And on December 7, Japanese forces launched a surprise attack on the American naval base in Pearl Harbor, Hawaii. This drew the United States into World War II.

Years of brutal fighting lay ahead. But the tide of the war was shifting. The combined might of the Soviet Union, the United States, Britain, and other Allied nations would defeat fascism. Italy was knocked out of the war in September 1943. Germany finally surrendered on May 8, 1945.

Japan, the third member of the Axis, fought on until August. By that time, the war that Hitler had started six years earlier with the invasion of Poland had claimed some 60 million lives.

That number is so staggering that it can be hard to appreciate the loss in human terms. But imagine if every man, woman, and child in the two largest U.S. states—California and Texas—were suddenly gone. That loss would be about the same as the death toll in World War II.

Beyond the shocking number of people killed, the sheer evil that fascism unleashed is difficult to comprehend. In the brutal and militaristic societies that fascism created, people willingly followed their leaders to unimaginably dark places. In Germany, otherwise ordinary people were enlisted into the wholesale slaughter of defenseless civilians, including children. Germans who weren't actively involved in the Holocaust managed to ignore the genocide occurring in their midst.

It's hard to imagine a more discredited political philosophy or system of government than fascism. And yet, small numbers of people still champion some of its ideas. In the United States and Europe, for example, neo-Nazi groups continue to rail against Jews and people of color. They continue to promote white racial supremacy. They continue, in some cases, to call for the violent overthrow of their countries' democratic governments.

Society ignores the pull of fascism at its own risk.

CHAPTER NOTES

p. 11:   "Either the government will . . ." Robert Ergang, *Europe in Our Time: 1914 to the Present*, 3rd ed. (Boston: D. C. Heath & Co, 1958), 238.

p. 18:   "The Aryan gave up . . ." William L. Shirer, *The Rise and Fall of the Third Reich: A History of Nazi Germany* (New York: Simon & Schuster Paperbacks, 1990), 87.

p. 19:   "highest species of humanity . . ." Ibid., 88.

p. 21:   "Feelings have to take . . ." Historian Q&A with Martin Kitchen, for *The Man Behind Hitler*, PBS *American Experience*. http://www.pbs.org/wgbh/amex/goebbels/sfeature/reich.html

p. 23:   "The only person who is still . . ." Hannah Arendt, *Totalitarianism: Part Three of the Origins of Totalitarianism* (Orlando, FL: Harcourt, Inc.: 1976), 37.

p. 23:   "The Fascist conception . . ." Benito Mussolini and Giovanni Gentile, "The Doctrine of Fascism" (1932). http://www.worldfuturefund.org/wffmaster/reading/germany/mussolini.htm

p. 23:   "Everything in the State . . ." Thomas Sowell, *Intellectuals in Society* (New York: Basic Books, 2009), 97.

p. 25:   "War is to men . . ." Robert O. Paxton, *The Anatomy of Fascism* (New York: Vintage Books, 2005), 156.

p. 25:   "War is inalienable . . ." Stanley G. Payne, *Fascism in Spain, 1923–1937* (Madison: University of Wisconsin Press, 1999), 154.

p. 25:   "Those who want to live . . ." Joseph W. Bendersky, *A History of Nazi Germany: 1919–1945* (Chicago: Rowman & Littlefield, 2000), 24.

p. 29:   "The state should retain supervision . . ." Sheldon Richman, "Fascism," in *The Concise Encyclopedia of Economics*. http://www.econlib.org/library/Enc/Fascism.html

p. 29:   "tended to be driven . . ." Paxton, *Anatomy of Fascism*, 145.

p. 37:   "With pride we see . . ." David Jablonsky, *Churchill and Hitler: Essays on the Political-Military Direction of Total War* (Ilford, Essex, England: Frank Cass & Co., 1994), 22.

p. 42:   "nation-corrupting . . ." United States Holocaust Memorial Museum, "Fighting the Fires of Hate: America and the Nazi Book Burnings" (online exhibit). http://www.ushmm.org/museum/exhibit/online/book-burning/burning.php

p. 42:   "a stronghold of the German . . ." Emmanuel Faye, *Heidegger: The Introduction of Nazism into Philosophy* (New Haven, CT: Yale University Press, 2009), 55.

p. 43:   "The age of arrogant . . ." United States Holocaust Memorial Museum, "Fighting the Fires of Hate."

p. 45:   "Italy at last has . . ." "World War: Destructible Power," *Time* (Aug. 4, 1941). http://www.time.com/time/magazine/article/0,9171,884366,00.html

p. 50:   "I believe it is peace . . ." "Return from Munich," *Guardian* (Oct. 1, 1938). http://www.guardian.co.uk/world/1938/oct/01/secondworldwar.fromthearchive

p. 51:   "Our enemies . . ." Paul Callan, "History's Biggest Lie," Express.co.uk (Sept. 5, 2008). http://www.express.co.uk/posts/view/60038/History-s-biggest-lie

CHRONOLOGY

1914–18: World War I.

1919: Benito Mussolini cofounds the Fascio Italiani di Combattimento (Italian Combat Leagues), the forerunner of Italy's Fascist Party. The German Workers' Party, which will become the Nazi Party, is founded.

1922: Mussolini becomes prime minister of Italy after the March on Rome.

1923: Adolf Hitler leads the unsuccessful Beer Hall Putsch in Germany.

1925: The first volume of Hitler's memoir, *Mein Kampf* ("My Struggle"), is published.

1933: In January, Hitler becomes chancellor of Germany.

1936: The Spanish civil war begins.

1939: On September 1, German forces invade Poland, triggering World War II.

1941: Germany invades the Soviet Union. The United States enters World War II after the Japanese attack on Pearl Harbor.

1945: World War II ends with the surrender of Germany in May, and the surrender of Japan in August.

GLOSSARY

ANTI-SEMITISM—hostility toward or hatred of Jews.

ATROCITY—a barbaric act.

AUTHORITARIAN—favoring or demanding blind submission to authority.

COALITION—a temporary alliance of groups, such as political parties.

COMMUNISM—a political and economic system that champions the elimination of private property and common ownership of goods, for the benefit of all members of society.

COUP—the sudden overthrow of a government by a small group, often through violence.

MANIFESTO—a written statement of political views or principles.

PARAMILITARY—relating to a force organized along military lines but not composed of official soldiers.

PROPAGANDA—information, often of a false or misleading nature, designed to get people to support the group spreading the information.

REPARATIONS—payments made by a defeated country, to compensate for damages done in the course of a war.

SOCIALISM—an economic system that is based on cooperation rather than competition and that utilizes centralized planning and distribution, controlled by the government.

TREASON—the crime of betraying one's country.

FURTHER READING

BOOKS FOR STUDENTS:

Corrigan, Jim. *Causes of World War II*. Stockton, NJ: OTTN Publishing, 2005.

Roberts, Jeremy. *Benito Mussolini*. Minneapolis: Lerner Publishing Group, 2005.

BOOKS FOR OLDER READERS:

Griffin, Roger (editor). *Fascism*. Oxford, UK: Oxford University Press, 1995.

Paxton, Robert O. *The Anatomy of Fascism*. New York: Alfred A. Knopf, 2004.

Payne, Stanley G. *A History of Fascism, 1914–1945*. London: UCL Press, 1995.

INTERNET RESOURCES

http://www.worldfuturefund.org/wffmaster/reading/germany/mussolini.htm

"The Doctrine of Fascism," the translation of a 1932 article by Benito Mussolini and Giovanni Gentile that sought to explain the principles of fascism.

http://www.ushmm.org

Website of the United States Holocaust Memorial Museum.

http://orwell.ru/library/articles/As_I_Please/english/efasc

In this short 1944 essay, the British writer George Orwell attempted to answer the question What is fascism?

http://specialcollections.library.wisc.edu/exhibits/Fascism/

"Italian Life Under Fascism," a virtual exhibit from the University of Madison–Wisconsin.

INDEX

anti-Semitism. *See* Jewish people
Aryan race, 18–19, 24, 26, 31
    See also racial groups
Austria, 48–49

Beer Hall Putsch, 16–17
Bismarck, Otto von, 26
Blackshirts, 9–12, 13–14, 25
book burning, 42–43
Brownshirts. *See* Sturmabteilung (SA)
Brüning, Heinrich, 35

Chamberlain, Neville, 49–50, *51*, 53
Chile, 44
civil war, Spanish, 46–47
communism, 8, 11, 12, 18, 22, 27, 33,
    34–35, 42, 46, 54
concentration camps, 39–40, *52*, 53,
    56–57
Czechoslovakia, 49–50, 53

Daladier, Édouard, 50, *51*
D'Annunzio, Gabriele, *9*

economic policy ("third way"), 27–29
Estado Novo (New State), 41, 44
Ethiopia, 45

Facta, Luigi, 11, 12
Falange Party (Spain), 25, 46
fasces (symbol), 10
Fasci Italiani di Combattimento
    (Italian Combat Leagues), 9–10
fascism, 9–11, 20–22, 26
    characteristics of, 21, 22–25,
        27–28, 44–45, 55
    and economic policy, 27–29
    in number of states worldwide,
        20, 44–45
    See also Hitler, Adolf; Mussolini,
        Benito
Fascist Manifesto of 1919, 10
Fatherland Front, 48–49
Franco, Francisco, 22, 46–47

Gentile, Giovanni, 23
German Student Association, 42
Germany, 22, 26, 41, 45, 47, 48–50
    and the Beer Hall Putsch, 16–17
    and economic policy, 29, 31–32

and politics, 30, 32–38, 39
    and the Weimar Republic, 16, 17,
        19, 32–33, 38
    and World War I, 14–16
    and World War II, 53–55, 56–57
    See also Hitler, Adolf
Gestapo, 22, 44
Giolitti, Giovanni, 11
Goebbels, Joseph, 21, 34–35, 40, 43

Hess, Rudolf, 18, 37
Hindenburg, Paul von, 32, 33, 35,
    36–38, 39
Hirohito (Emperor), 55
Hitler, Adolf, 16–17, *21*, 25, 26, *45*,
    49, *51*, 54
    anti-Semitism of, 14, 18–19, 31,
        40
    and economic policy, 29
    and *Mein Kampf*, 18–19
    and the Munich Agreement,
        50–51, 53
    and politics, 30, 33–35, 36–38
    and racial groupings, 18–19
    and the Sudetenland, 49–51
    and World War I, 14, *15*
    See also Nazi Party
Hitler Youth, *28*, 30–31, 52–53
Holocaust, 56–57

Italy, 22, 26, 45, 47, 48, 49
    and economic policy, 28, 29
    election laws in, 13–14
    and the founding of the Fascist
        movement, 9–11
    and the Manifesto of Race, 51–52
    and the March on Rome, 7–8,
        11–13
    and World War I, 8–9, 10
    and World War II, 53–54, 55, 57
    See also Mussolini, Benito

Japan, 54, 55, 57
Jewish people, 14, 16, 18, 24, 26, 31,
    33, *52*
    and concentration camps, 39–40,
        52, 53, 56–57
    and the Manifesto of Race, 51–52
    and the Nuremberg Laws, 41
    and "official anti-Semitism,"

40–41

Kristallnacht, 52–53

League of German Girls, 30–31
Ley, Robert, 23

Manifesto of Race, 51–52
March on Rome, 7–8, 11–13
Mein Kampf (Hitler), 18–19
Mosley, Oswald, 44
Movimiento Nacional Socialista
    (National Socialist Movement),
    44
Munich Agreement, 50–51, 53
Mussolini, Benito, *6*, 9, *21*, 24, 25, 26,
    45, *51*, 53, 54
    and economic policy, 28
    as "Il Duce," 14
    and the Manifesto of Race, 51–52
    and the March on Rome, 7–8,
        11–13
    and the Munich Agreement, 50
    and the Partito Nazionale
        Fascista, 11
    and supremacy of the state, 23
    See also Italy

National Front (Spain), 46–47
National Socialist German Workers
    Party. *See* Nazi Party
nationalism, 10, 23–25, 26, 33
Nazi Party, 16–17, 18, 19, *24*, 26, 41
    in Austria, 49
    and book burning, 42–43
    and concentration camps, 39–40,
        52, 53, 56–57
    and economic policy, 29
    and the Hitler Youth, *28*, 30–31,
        52–53
    and politics, 30, 33–38, 39
    and propaganda, 21, *32*, 34–35,
        42
    and "racial hygiene," 50
    and World War II, 53–54, 55,
        56–57
    See also Germany; Hitler, Adolf
Nuremberg Laws, 41

"Pact of Steel," 54

Numbers in **bold italics** refer to captions.

Papen, Franz von, 35–36, 37, 38
Partito Nazionale Fascista (National Fascist Party), 11, 13–14
Paxton, Robert O., 29
Poland, 53, 54–55
Popular Front (Spain), 46
Portugal, 22, 41, 44, 47
Primo de Rivera, José Antonio, 25
propaganda, 21, 22, *32*, 34–35, 42

racial groups, 18–19, 23–24
  Aryans, 18–19, 24, 26, 31
    and the Manifesto of Race, 51–52
    and the Nuremberg Laws, 41
    See also Jewish people
Reichstag (German parliament), 30, 32–38, *40*

See also Germany
Rome-Berlin Axis, 48, 49

Salazar, António de Oliveira, 22, 41, 44
Schleicher, Kurt von, 35–36, 37, 38
Schuschnigg, Kurt, 49
Schutzstaffel (SS), 31, 35, 36, 52–53, 56
secret police, 22
socialism, 11, 42
Soviet Union, 54, 56, 57
Spain, 22, 25, 46–47
squadristi. *See* Blackshirts
Sturmabteilung (SA), 14, 16, 17, *24*, 25, *27*, 31, 34, 35, 36, 38
Sudetenland, 49–50

totalitarianism, 23

Treaty of Versailles, 14, 16, 41
Ustasha, 55–56

Victor Emmanuel III (King), 12–13

Weimar Republic, 16, 17, 19, 32–33, 38
  See also Germany
Wilhelm II (Kaiser), 15
World War I, 8–9, 10, 14–16
World War II, 53–57

CONTRIBUTORS

Senior Consulting Editor **TIMOTHY J. COLTON** is Morris and Anna Feldberg Professor of Government and Russian Studies and is the chair of the Department of Government at Harvard University. His books include *The Dilemma of Reform in the Soviet Union* (1986); *Moscow: Governing the Socialist Metropolis* (1995), which was named best scholarly book in government and political science by the Association of American Publishers; *Transitional Citizens: Voters and What Influences Them in the New Russia* (2000); and *Popular Choice and Managed Democracy: The Russian Elections of 1999 and 2000* (with Michael McFaul, 2003). Dr. Colton is a member of the editorial board of World Politics and Post-Soviet Affairs.

SETH H. PULDITOR, a freelance writer based in New York, is the author of several books for young adults. His interests include history, politics, and music.